STARTERS

The Sea

Claire Llewellyn

an imprint of Hodder Children's Books

Text copyright © Claire Llewellyn 2003

Consultant: Carol Ballard
Language consultant: Andrew Burrell
Design: Perry Tate Design

Published in Great Britain in 2003
by Hodder Wayland, an imprint of
Hodder Children's Books

The publishers would like to thank the following for allowing us to reproduce their
pictures in this book: Oxford Scientific Films; cover, title page, 5 (top), 15-16
(bottom), 17, 19 / Science Photo Library; 6-7, 10 /11 (top), 16 (top) / Hodder
Wayland picture library; 4,5 (bottom) / Still Pictures; 8 / Ecoscene; contents page,
9-10 (top), 18, 20 / Bruce Coleman; 11 (middle), 12 (bottom), 13 / NHPA; 12 (top) /
Corbis; 14, 21-23

A Catalogue record for this book is available from the British Library.

ISBN: 0750244178

Printed and bound in Singapore

Hodder Children's Books
A division of Hodder Headline Limited
338 Euston Road, London NW1 3BH

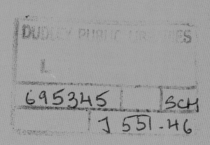

Contents

A day by the sea

A day by the sea is so much fun – is there anyone who doesn't enjoy it? You can paddle, swim and fish in the sea, ski, surf and sail on it.

But few of us dive beneath the waves or know much about this hidden world.

The world's oceans

The sea is truly **enormous**. It covers so much of the Earth's surface that, from Space, our planet looks blue.

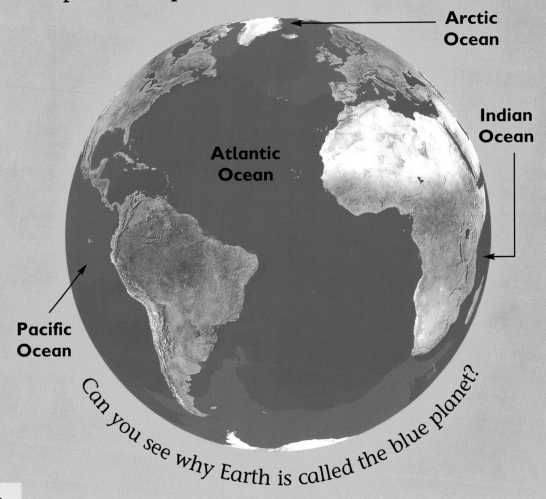

Arctic Ocean

Indian Ocean

Atlantic Ocean

Pacific Ocean

Can you see why Earth is called the blue planet?

The sea is made up of four huge oceans, which flow into one another. Some of these oceans are warm. Others are so cold that they are covered with ice.

Giant icebergs float in the Arctic Ocean.

The sea is always on the move. Strong winds blow across its surface, making waves that CRASH against the shore.

The sea moves in another way, too. Twice a day, it RISES up the shore and twice a day, it FALLS. We call this high and low tide.

high tide

low tide

Life in the sea

The sea is full of life.
It is home to many
different animals
and plants.

Coral reefs grow in warm, clean, shallow seas.

Starfish
are the only animals
with five arms.

Sea slugs come
in amazing shapes
and colours.

Watch out for jellyfish. They can give you a nasty sting!

A body for the sea

Sea animals look very different from animals that live on land. Most have a **smooth**, streamlined shape that glides easily through the water.

The barracuda is one of the fastest fish in the sea.

A squid moves gracefully through the water.

And, instead of arms and legs or hoofs and claws, they have powerful flippers and fins.

A seal's body is streamlined for life in the sea.

Smooth skin

Tail works as a paddle

Flippers help the seal to change direction

Breathing in water

All animals need oxygen to stay alive. There is oxygen in the air, but there is also oxygen in the sea.

Animals that breathe in the air take in oxygen through their lungs. Animals that breathe under water take in oxygen through their gills.

A fish has gills on the side of its head.

gills

Sea turtles do not have gills. They can only breathe in the air.

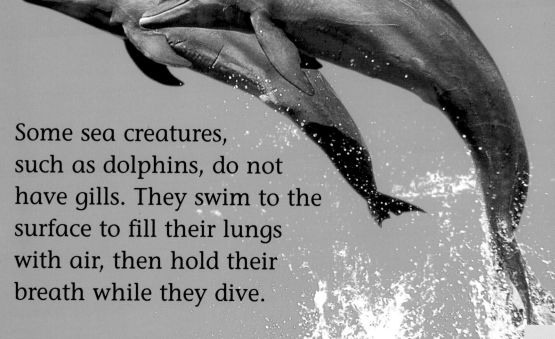

Some sea creatures, such as dolphins, do not have gills. They swim to the surface to fill their lungs with air, then hold their breath while they dive.

Feeding time

Some sea creatures feed on plants, but many of them feed on each other!

Sharks can kill animals as big as seals.

Octopuses use their long arms to catch small animals, such as crabs.

Animals don't want to be eaten. The porcupine fish protects itself with prickly spines.

Small fish stick together in huge groups called shoals.

The sea provides us with food. Every day, fishermen set out with nets, hooks and spears to catch fish, octopus, shellfish and other tasty foods.

We are taking so much from the sea, that some creatures could soon die out.

Many birds also depend on the sea. They have learned to dive into the water and catch fish with their beaks.

A puffin packs lots of fish in its beak.

A pelican dives into the water at high speed.

Ships and boats

Many kinds of ships and boats sail on the sea. Some carry passengers, but most of them carry cargo, such as timber, bananas or oil.

Huge tankers carry oil across the sea.

Other boats have a special use. Lifeboats are called out in stormy weather to rescue people at sea.

Lifeboats are strong, safe – and very fast!

Exploring the seabed

The sea can be very dangerous.
Over the years, thousands of ships
have SUNK in stormy seas.
Divers explore the ocean
floor, searching for these
long-lost wrecks.

Though people have always explored the land, the seabed is largely unknown. Who knows what secrets are still to be found at the bottom of the sea?

Glossary and index

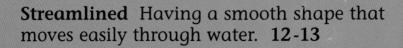

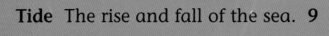